Sports Illustrated KIDS

THE ULTIMATE GUIDE TO PRO BASEBALL TEAMS

by Nate LeBoutillier

CAPSTONE PRESS
a capstone imprint

Sports Illustrated KIDS Ultimate Pro Team Guides are published by Capstone Press, 151 Good Counsel Drive, P.O. Box 669, Mankato, Minnesota 56002. www.capstonepub.com

For information regarding permission, write to Capstone Press, 151 Good Counsel Drive, P.O. Box 669, Dept. R, Mankato, Minnesota 56002.

Sports Illustrated KIDS is a trademark of Time, Inc. Used with permission.

Printed in the United States of America in North Mankato, Minnesota.

032010
005740CGF10

Books published by Capstone Press are manufactured with paper containing at least 10 percent post-consumer waste.

Library of Congress Cataloging-in-Publication Data
LeBoutillier, Nate.
  The ultimate guide to pro baseball teams / by Nate LeBoutillier.
    p. cm.—(Sports illustrated KIDS. Ultimate pro guides)
  Includes index.
ISBN 978-1-4296-4820-2 (library binding)
ISBN 978-1-4296-5640-5 (paperback)
1. Baseball teams—United States—Juvenile literature.
2. Baseball teams—Ontario—Toronto—Juvenile
literature. 3. Baseball—United States—Juvenile literature.
4. Baseball—Ontario—Toronto—Juvenile literature.
I. Title. II. Series.
GV875.A1L42 2010
796.357'64—dc22   2010012056

Editorial Credits: Anthony Wacholtz, editor; Tracy Davies, designer; Eric Gohl, media researcher; Laura Manthe, production specialist

Image Credits: BigStockPhoto.com: Eric Broder Van Dyke, 45 (b); Eric Gohl, 39 (b), 64 (t); Getty Images Inc.: G Flume, 65 (b); iStockphoto: Leo Kowal (field), cover, back cover, 2, 66–67, 68–69, 70–71, Randy Plett Photographs (baseball), cover, back cover, 1, 68; Jake Keegan, 55 (b); Library of Congress, 17 (b), 20 (b), 25 (t), 43 (b), 48 (b); Newscom: 37 (t), 63 (b), Icon SMI/Joe Robbins, 61 (t), Icon SMI/*Sporting News*/Malcolm Emmons, 39 (t); Shutterstock: Antony McAulay (lights), cover, Christopher Penler, 13 (b), doodle (shattered glass), back cover, 68, Ken Inness, 62 (b), M.E. Mulder, design element, Robert Pernell, 48 (t), Tomasz Sowinski, design element, Vallentin Vassileff, cover (bl); *Sports Illustrated*: Al Tielemans, cover (br), 6 (b), 10 (b), 20 (t), 28 (t), 46 (all), 52 (t), 67 (background right), Bill Frakes, 58 (b), Bob Rosato, 8 (b), 21 (t), 58 (t), 60 (t), Chuck Solomon, 1, 15 (b), 18 (t), 22 (all), 27 (b), 28 (b), 33 (t), 40 (b), 43 (t), 61 (b), 63 (t), Damian Strohmeyer, 54 (b), 59 (b), 67 (background left), David E. Klutho, 6 (t), 15 (t), 29 (b), 52 (b), 56 (t), 60 (b), 66 (background right), Heinz Kluetmeier, 11 (t), 31 (b), 38 (t), 45 (t), 49 (t), 59 (t), 65 (t), John Biever, cover (bm), 4–5, 7 (all), 14 (t), 16 (t), 23 (b), 24 (b), 25 (t), 29 (t), 36 (all), 38 (b), 42 (t), 55 (t), 66 (background left & middle), 67 (background middle), John D. Hanlon, 44 (b), John G. Zimmerman, 8 (t), 9 (t), 12 (b), 35 (t), 42 (b), 53 (t), John Iacono, 9 (b), 10 (t), 12 (t), 16 (b), 21 (b), 24 (t), 26 (t), 30 (b), 40 (t), 41 (t), 47 (all), 62 (t), John W. McDonough, 32 (t), 50 (all), 67 (front), Lane Stewart, 13 (t), Manny Millan, 31 (t), 37 (b), 57 (b), Mark Kauffman, 35 (b), 49 (b), 57 (t), Peter Read Miller, 44 (t), Richard Meek, 17 (t), 34 (b), Robert Beck, 2, 14 (b), 23 (t), 27 (t), 30 (t), 32 (b), 34 (t), 51 (all), 53 (b), 54 (t), 56 (b), Simon Bruty, 26 (b), 64 (b), V.J. Lovero, 33 (b), 41 (b), Walter Iooss Jr., 18 (b), 19 (all); Wikipedia: Ed Brown, 11 (b).

TABLE OF CONTENTS

THE NATIONAL PASTIME

Hitting a small, fast-traveling ball with a narrow stick is one of the toughest acts to learn in any sport. Add in running, catching, and throwing, and there are a lot of things for a baseball player to master. Baseball is nicknamed "America's pastime," and fans love watching players from their favorite teams take the field throughout the summer to put on a show of athleticism.

The game was created based on rules from cricket, a game played in England dating back to the 1500s. The sport evolved over the next few centuries until teams began

organizing in the mid-19th century in America. By the late-1800s professional baseball organizations were in full swing.

With 30 teams at the pro level, Major League Baseball is played across the United States and into Canada. Every autumn fans and players look forward to the World Series, where the top team from the American League squares off against the champion of the National League. The two teams clash in a best of seven series, knowing it will be a long winter before the next season starts.

All regular season stats are through the 2009 season.

ARIZONA DIAMONDBACKS

First Season: 1998

Franchise Record: 970–974
Home Field: Chase Field
(49,033 capacity) in Phoenix, Arizona

CHAMPIONSHIP
2001

2001 World Series celebration

The state of Arizona had been the spring training location for several major league teams before the Diamondbacks became an expansion team in 1998. The next season they won 100 games and made the playoffs. And then in just their fourth season, the D-backs shocked the baseball world by bringing home the World Series title in 2001. It was the fastest an expansion team had ever gone from creation to championship.

Legends & Stars

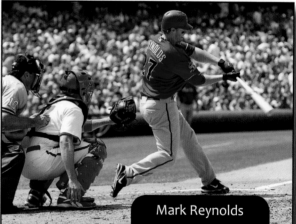
Mark Reynolds

Craig Counsell	IF	2000–2003, 2005–2006	Utility man played all four infield positions for Arizona
Luis Gonzalez	LF	1999–2006	Batted .325 with 57 home runs and 142 RBIs in 2001
Randy Johnson	SP	1999–2004, 2007–2008	From 1999 to 2002, Johnson won four consecutive NL Cy Young awards and was co-MVP of the 2001 World Series
Mark Reynolds	3B	2007–present	Up-and-coming power star had 44 homers in 2009
Curt Schilling	SP	2000–2003	Co-MVP of 2001 World Series went 58–28 in three and a half seasons for Arizona
Justin Upton	OF	2007–present	Young outfielder became an All-Star in 2009

By the Numbers

HITS	**Luis Gonzalez** 1999–2006 1,337		WINS	**Randy Johnson** 1999–2004, 2007–2008 118
HOME RUNS	**Luis Gonzalez** 224		Ks	**Randy Johnson** 2,077
STEALS	**Tony Womack** 1999–2003 182		SAVES	**Jose Valverde** 2003–2007 98

Statewide Appeal

Diamondbacks owner Jerry Colangelo had the choice of what the team would be named. Team officials liked the fan-submitted idea of the diamondback—a poisonous snake native to the southwestern United States. Colangelo also owned the NBA team the Phoenix Suns, so the Phoenix Diamondbacks seemed like a good fit. However, he decided on the Arizona Diamondbacks instead so the team would draw more fans.

Randy Johnson (left) and Curt Schilling

Mature Winners

To become World Series champions in only four years, the Diamondbacks took an unusual approach to building a team. They decided to build around veterans rather than youth. In 2001 the D-backs' entire starting lineup and two star pitchers—Randy Johnson and Curt Schilling—were all in their 30s.

ATLANTA BRAVES

First Season: 1876

Franchise Record: 9,854–9,883–154
Home Field: Turner Field
(50,096 capacity) in Atlanta, Georgia

CHAMPIONSHIPS
1914, 1957, 1995

The Braves' long history started in 1876 in Boston, where they were known as the Red Caps. Many name changes followed, including Beaneaters, Doves, Rustlers, Bees, and finally Braves. The team played in Milwaukee, Wisconsin, from 1953 until 1965, featuring one of the best home run hitters of all time: Hank Aaron. In 1966 the Braves began play in Atlanta. They won the World Series title in 1995 in the midst of a major league record 14 straight playoff appearances.

The Milwaukee Braves celebrate after winning the 1957 World Series.

Legends & Stars

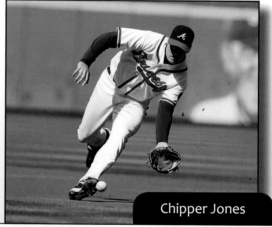

Chipper Jones

Hank Aaron	RF	1954–1974	MLB's all-time leader in home runs and RBIs when he retired
Chipper Jones	3B	1993–present	Braves veteran has been an anchor at third base
Greg Maddux	SP	1993–2003	Won 18 Gold Gloves and 4 NL Cy Young awards
Brian McCann	C	2005–present	Solid backstop was selected to the All-Star Game four straight years (2006–2009)
Dale Murphy	OF	1976–1990	Won back-to-back NL MVP awards in 1982 and 1983 and took home five Gold Gloves
Phil Niekro	P	1966–1983, 1987	His dancing knuckleball kept him in the game until he was 48
Warren Spahn	P	1942, 1946–1964	Won 20 or more games 13 times

By the Numbers

HITS	**Hank Aaron** 1954–1974 3,600		**WINS**	**Warren Spahn** 1942, 1946–1964 356
HOME RUNS	**Hank Aaron** 733		**Ks**	**John Smoltz** 1988–2008 3,011
STEALS	**Herman Long** 1890–1902 434		**SAVES**	**John Smoltz** 154

Ted's Team

The Atlanta Braves were nicknamed "America's Team" by Turner Broadcasting System, a cable TV network that carried Braves ballgames from 1975 to 2007. The Braves were Ted Turner's team—he owned the Braves and TBS. The national TV coverage for 32 years greatly increased the Braves' fan base.

Ted Turner with the 1995 World Series trophy

Babe's Swan Song

Although best remembered as a New York Yankees' star, slugger Babe Ruth played his final baseball season with the Boston Braves. Appearing in just 28 games in the 1935 season, the 40-year-old "Bambino" batted a measly .181. He launched six home runs that summer to bring his major league total to 714.

BALTIMORE ORIOLES

Franchise Record: 8,017–8,880–110

Home Field: Oriole Park at Camden Yards

(48,876 capacity) in Baltimore, Maryland

CHAMPIONSHIPS
1929, 1939, 1941, 1970, 1972

First Season: 1901

Professional baseball started in 1901 in Baltimore, Maryland. That year a team called the Baltimore Orioles was a charter member of the eight-team American League. Two years later the team moved to New York and eventually became the New York Yankees. The Baltimore Orioles of today started in 1901 from another charter AL team: the Milwaukee Brewers. In 1902 the Brewers moved to St. Louis, Missouri, and became the Browns. They migrated to Baltimore in 1953 to become the Orioles.

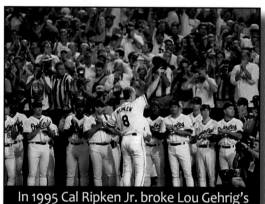
In 1995 Cal Ripken Jr. broke Lou Gehrig's consecutive game streak of 2,130 games.

Legends & Stars

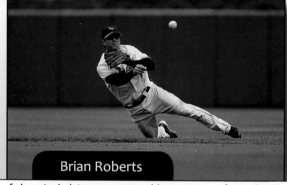
Brian Roberts

Eddie Murray	1B/DH	1977–1988, 1996	Powerful switch-hitter swatted home runs from both sides of the plate in the same game 11 times
Jim Palmer	P	1965–1984	Awarded three Cy Young awards and four Gold Gloves, made six All-Star appearances, and won two World Series titles
Cal Ripken Jr.	SS	1981–2001	Most famous for Iron Man streak of 2,632 consecutive games played; won AL MVP in 1983 and 1991
Brian Roberts	2B	2001–present	Two-time All-Star is a top-of-the-order hitter and base stealer
Brooks Robinson	3B	1955–1977	16-time Gold Glove winner was awarded the 1964 AL MVP
Frank Robinson	OF	1966–1971	Won AL MVP in 1961 and 1966; managed the O's from 1988 to 1991
Matt Wieters	C	2009–present	Baltimore's catcher of the future played a solid rookie season

By the Numbers

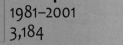

HITS	**Cal Ripken Jr.** 1981–2001 3,184	**WINS**	**Jim Palmer** 1965–1984 268
HOME RUNS	**Cal Ripken Jr.** 431	**Ks**	**Jim Palmer** 2,212
STEALS	**George Sisler** 1915–1927 351	**SAVES**	**Gregg Olson** 1988–1993 160

Home of the Babe

Though the famous slugger Babe Ruth did the majority of his baseball playing in New York for the Yankees, he was born in Baltimore. The Orioles display a statue of Ruth outside their stadium at Camden Yards.

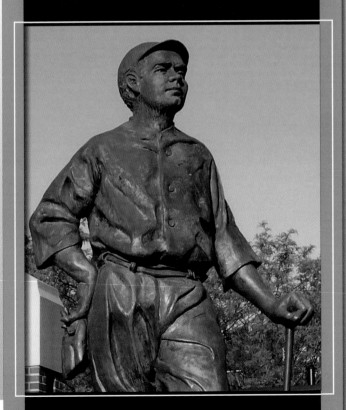

Family Reunion

When Cal Ripken Sr. became the manager of the Orioles in 1987, he was the third Ripken in the major league club. Sons Billy (second base) and Cal Jr. (shortstop) turned many double plays in the field under their father's leadership, though the team finished 67–95.

11

BOSTON RED SOX

Franchise Record: 8,730–8,160–83
Home Field: Fenway Park
(36,984 capacity) in Boston, Massachusetts

CHAMPIONSHIPS
1903, 1912, 1915, 1916, 1918, 2004, 2007

First Season: 1901

The Boston Americans were one of the eight charter members of the American League in 1901 and were renamed the Red Sox in 1908. The team found great success early in the century with four World Series titles before World War I. Then began a long streak without a championship that finally ended in 2004. Many Red Sox fans attributed this dry spell to the Red Sox trading away the legendary Babe Ruth to the Yankees in 1919, which prompted the "Curse of the Bambino."

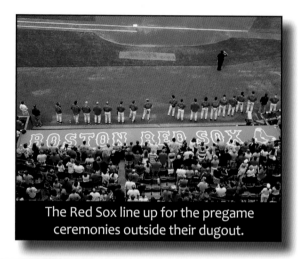
The Red Sox line up for the pregame ceremonies outside their dugout.

Legends & Stars

Ted Williams

Wade Boggs	3B	1982–1992	Singles-hitting third basemen had superstition of eating chicken before every game
Roger Clemens	SP	1984–1996	In 1986 dominant fastball pitcher went 24–4, won the Cy Young Award and MVP, and struck out 20 batters in a single game
Jonathan Papelbon	RP	2005–present	Fireballing closer is a fan favorite at Fenway
Jim Rice	OF/DH	1974–1989	In 1978 Rice batted .315, slugged 46 homers, and had 139 RBIs to win the AL MVP
Ted Williams	OF	1939–1942, 1946–1960	"The Splendid Splinter" batted above .400 four times; career was interrupted for three seasons by military service in World War II
Carl Yastrzemski	1B/OF	1961–1983	"Yaz" played 22 seasons and won the AL MVP in 1967

By the Numbers

HITS	**Carl Yastrzemski** 1961–1983 3,419	**WINS**	**Roger Clemens** 1984–1996 **Cy Young** 1901–1908 192 each
HOME RUNS	**Ted Williams** 1939–1942, 1946–1960 521	**Ks**	**Roger Clemens** 2,590
STEALS	**Harry Hooper** 1909–1920 300	**SAVES**	**Jonathan Papelbon** 2005–present 151

The Green Monster

The left-field wall at Fenway Park can be a curse or a blessing for hitters. Known as the Green Monster, it is the tallest wall in any baseball stadium. Right-handed line-drive hitters have a hard time hitting over the Green Monster. Hitters who hit high fly balls may be rewarded with a home run on a hit that would be an out in many other parks. Down the foul line, the left-field wall is only about 310 feet (94 meters) from home plate.

The Green Monster is 37 feet (11 meters) tall.

Sweet Traditions

Neil Diamond's *Sweet Caroline* has become a tradition at Fenway Park. It was originally considered a good luck charm in 1998, when it was only played when the Red Sox were winning. Since 2002 the familiar song blares from the speakers after the top of the 8th inning at Red Sox home games.

13

CHICAGO CUBS

First Season: 1876

Franchise Record: 10,165–9,601–160
Home Field: Wrigley Field
(41,118 capacity) in Chicago, Illinois

CHAMPIONSHIPS
1907, 1908

One of the oldest franchises in pro baseball started in the National League in 1876 as the White Stockings. The team was renamed the Colts and Orphans before becoming the Cubs in 1903, which they've been known as ever since. After winning back-to-back World Series in 1907 and 1908, the Cubs have gone more than 100 years without a championship.

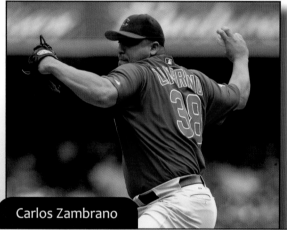
Derrek Lee

Legends & Stars

Carlos Zambrano

Ernie Banks	SS/1B	1953–1971	"Mr. Cub" won back-to-back NL MVPs in 1958 and 1959
Ferguson "Fergie" Jenkins	SP	1966–73, 1982–1983	Won 20 games or more in six seasons for the Cubs and took home the NL Cy Young Award in 1971
Derrek Lee	1B	2004–present	Power and average hitter won NL batting title with a .335 batting average in 2005
Ryne Sandberg	2B	1982–1994, 1996–1997	"Ryno" stacked up nine Gold Gloves to go with an NL MVP in 1984
Ron Santo	3B	1960–1973	Nine-time NL All-Star won five Gold Gloves
Billy Williams	LF	1959–1974	Sweet-swinging outfielder hit for both power and average
Carlos Zambrano	SP	2001–present	Fiery power pitcher has been selected to three All-Star games

By the Numbers

HITS	Cap Anson 1876–1897 3,012	**WINS**	Charlie Root 1926–1941 201	
HOME RUNS	Sammy Sosa 1992–2004 545	**Ks**	Fergie Jenkins 1966–73, 1982–1983 2,038	
STEALS	Frank Chance 1898–1912 400	**SAVES**	Lee Smith 1980–1987 180	

Curse of the Goat

Before Game 4 of the 1945 World Series in Chicago, local tavern owner Billy Sianis was invited onto the field. He brought his pet goat, which wore a sign around its neck that said, "We got Detroit's Goat." When Sianis and his goat went to the stands to watch the game, the goat's foul smell led to complaints from the fans. Sianis and his goat were eventually ejected. So began the curse of the goat—the Cubs haven't been to the World Series since.

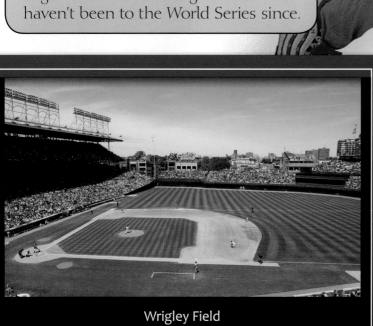

Wrigley Field

Landmark Ballpark

The Cubs play in the National League's oldest stadium. Built in 1914, Wrigley Field features an outfield wall covered in ivy. Baseball tourists have made it one of the most visited ballparks in America.

CHICAGO WHITE SOX

Franchise Record: 8,540–8,339–103
Home Field: U.S. Cellular Field
(40,615 capacity) in Chicago, Illinois

CHAMPIONSHIPS
1906, 1917, 2005

First Season: 1901

The White Sox were one of the eight charter members of the American League in 1901. In 1906 the Sox beat their crosstown rivals, the Cubs, in the 1906 World Series. That was the last time the Sox faced the Cubs until interleague regular season play began in 1997. After an 88-year drought, the White Sox took home their third title in 2005.

2005 World Series champions

Legends & Stars

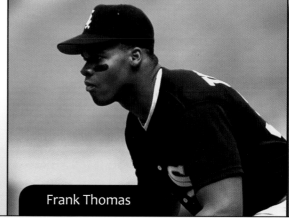

Frank Thomas

Luke Appling	SS	1930–1950	White Sox regular for 21 seasons captured AL batting titles in 1936 and 1943
Mark Buehrle	SP	2000–present	In 2009 Buehrle threw the 18th perfect game in MLB history
Carlton Fisk	C	1981–1993	One of the most reliable backstops of all time, Fisk played 13 seasons in Chicago and 11 seasons in Boston
Nellie Fox	2B	1950–1963	Three-time Gold Glove winner earned the AL MVP award in 1959
Minnie Minoso	LF	1951–1957, 1960–1961, 1976, 1980	"The Cuban Comet" set MLB record by playing in five decades for four different teams
Alexei Ramirez	SS	2008–present	Wide-range shortstop has both speed and power
Frank Thomas	1B/DH	1990–2005	"The Big Hurt" intimidated pitchers with a strong swing and an eagle eye, leading the majors in walks three times

By the Numbers

HITS	**Luke Appling** 1930–1950 2,749		**WINS**	**Ted Lyons** 1923–1942 260	
HOME RUNS	**Frank Thomas** 1990–2005 448		**Ks**	**Billy Pierce** 1949–1961 1,796 ⟶	
STEALS	**Eddie Collins** 1915–1926 368		**SAVES**	**Bobby Thigpen** 1986–1993 201	

Disco Fever

On July 12, 1979, Sox owner Bill Veeck declared it to be Disco Demolition Night at Comiskey Park, longtime home of the team. Any fan who brought a disco record into the ballpark that night received admission to the doubleheader against the Detroit Tigers for just 98 cents. But after a large stack of records was blown up as part of the promotion following the first game, the jam-packed stadium's fans rioted and the second game was canceled.

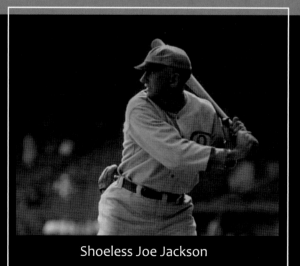

Shoeless Joe Jackson

A Case for Shoeless Joe

Though the 1919 White Sox were accused of purposely losing the World Series as part of a gambling scheme, "Shoeless" Joe Jackson batted .375 with no errors in the Fall Classic. Still, MLB suspended him from ever playing again after the 1920 season. He insisted on his innocence for the rest of his life. Whether Shoeless Joe should be inducted into the Hall of Fame is one of baseball's great debates.

CINCINNATI REDS

First Season: 1882

Franchise Record: 9,824–9,548–139
Home Field: Great American Ball Park (42,059 capacity) in Cincinnati, Ohio

CHAMPIONSHIPS
1919, 1940, 1975, 1976, 1990

Professional baseball in Cincinnati began in 1882 with the Red Stockings. In 1890 the team name was shortened to Reds, only to be lengthened to Redlegs for six seasons in the 1950s. In 1960 Reds became the team name again. In the 1970s the Reds were referred to as the "Big Red Machine" and won back-to-back World Series titles in 1975 and 1976.

Brandon Phillips

Legends & Stars

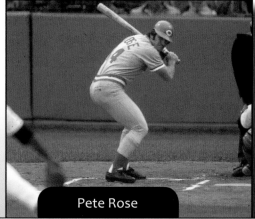

Pete Rose

Sparky Anderson		1970–1978	Managed the Reds to four World Series, winning two
Johnny Bench	C	1967–1983	Collected 10 Gold Gloves, 14 All-Star selections, and two NL MVP awards during a remarkable career
Dave Concepcion	SS	1970–1988	Nine-time All-Star was part of the Big Red Machine
Joe Morgan	2B	1972–1979	Defensive star won five Gold Gloves to go with NL MVP trophies in 1975 and 1976
Brandon Phillips	2B	2006–present	Second baseman has the ability to hit home runs and steal bases
Pete Rose	IF/OF	1963–1978, 1984–1986	Baseball's all-time hits leader; banned from MLB in 1989 for betting on baseball games
Joey Votto	1B	2007–present	Rising star first baseman aiming for above .300 average and 25 home runs per season

By the Numbers

HITS	**Pete Rose** 1963–1978, 1984–1986 3,358	**WINS**	**Eppa Rixey** 1921–1933 179
HOME RUNS	**Johnny Bench** 1967–1983 389	**Ks**	**Jim Maloney** 1960–1970 1,592
STEALS	**Joe Morgan** 1972–1979 406	**SAVES**	**Danny Graves** 1997–2005 182

Winning When It Counts

During the 1975 World Series, with the series tied at three, the Big Red Machine beat the Boston Red Sox in Game 7 at Fenway Park. That game started a winning trend in the Reds' World Series appearances. The following season Cincinnati swept the New York Yankees to become champions. The team didn't make it to the World Series again until 1990, when they played the heavily favored Oakland Athletics. Behind manager Lou Piniella and the pitching of Jose Rijo, the Reds took the series in four games.

The crowd goes wild after Tony Perez hits a home run in Game 7 of the 1975 World Series.

Big Red Machine

During the early 1970s, nobody played baseball like the Reds. Writer Bob Hertzel coined the nickname "Big Red Machine," which referred to Pete Rose, Joe Morgan, Johnny Bench, Tony Perez, Dave Concepcion, George Foster, Cesar Geronimo, and Ken Griffey Sr.

CLEVELAND INDIANS

First Season: 1901

Franchise Record: 8,622–8,274–91
Home Field: Progressive Field
(43,545 capacity) in Cleveland, Ohio

CHAMPIONSHIPS
1920, 1948

The Cleveland Blues were one of the charter teams in the American League in 1901. The team changed names to the Bronchos and the Naps before the Cleveland Indians stuck in 1915. The Indians won their first World Series title in 1920, and they won it again in 1948. One of the most famous pitchers of all time, Cy Young, was born near Cleveland in Gilmore, Ohio. He played for the Indians during the peak of his career.

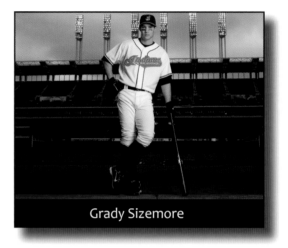
Grady Sizemore

Legends & Stars

Cy Young

Asdrubal Cabrera	SS	2007–present	Switch-hitter batted .308 in second full season
Bob Feller	SP	1936–1941, 1944–1956	The first MLB player to enlist in the military after the U.S. was bombed at Pearl Harbor in 1941; he threw three no-hitters during his career
Bob Lemon	SP	1941–1942, 1946–1958	Third baseman-turned-pitcher won 20 or more games seven times with the Indians
Grady Sizemore	OF	2004–present	Indians All-Star with a mix of speed and power has two Gold Gloves
Jim Thome	1B/DH	1991–2002	Powerful slugger hit 52 home runs in 2002 for the Indians
Early Wynn	SP	1949–1957, 1963	Intimidating fastballer pitched 23 seasons and won 300 games
Cy Young	SP	1890–1898, 1909–1911	Baseball's all-time leader in wins has pitching award named after him

By the Numbers

HITS	**Nap Lajoie** 1902–1914 2,046	
WINS	**Bob Feller** 1936–1941, 1944–1956 266	
HOME RUNS	**Jim Thome** 1991–2002 334	
Ks	**Bob Feller** 2,581	
STEALS	**Kenny Lofton** 1992–1996, 1998–2001, 2007 452	
SAVES	**Bob Wickman** 2000–2002, 2004–2006 139	

Two Outs Away

Despite a slow start to the 1997 season, the Indians ended with an 86–75 record and became division champions. After beating the New York Yankees and the Baltimore Orioles in the playoffs, they met the Florida Marlins in the World Series. The series was tied at three, and the Indians held a 2-1 lead in the ninth inning of Game 7. With two outs to go, closer Jose Mesa allowed the tying run, and the Marlins won the game and the series in the 11th inning.

Sandy Alomar Jr. hits a home run against the Yankees in the 1997 AL Championship Series.

Rare Card

In 1933 the Goudy Gum Company of Boston forgot to issue a baseball card of one of the majors' best players, Napoleon "Nap" Lajoie, a Cleveland infielder. Collectors wanting a Lajoie card could write to Goudy for a replacement. Today the rare card is valued at $25,000.

21

COLORADO ROCKIES

First Season: 1993

Franchise Record: 1,281–1,411
Home Field: Coors Field
(50,445 capacity) in Denver, Colorado

CHAMPIONSHIPS
None

Introduced to fans along with the Florida Marlins as expansion teams in 1993, the Rockies were a success in Denver from the very beginning. Hordes of fans turned out in the first season to set a major league record for season attendance. Canadian slugger Larry Walker was a fan favorite in the franchise's building years. In 2007 the Rockies made their first World Series appearance but were downed by the Boston Red Sox.

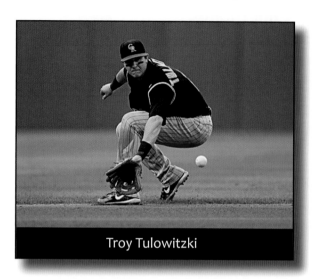
Troy Tulowitzki

Legends & Stars

Matt Holliday

Dante Bichette	OF	1993–1999	Four time All-Star was a hit with the Rockies
Andres Galarraga	1B	1993–1997	"Big Cat" hit a career-high .370 in 1993 to win the NL batting title
Todd Helton	1B	1997–present	Won 2000 NL batting title with an amazing .372 average
Matt Holliday	LF	2004–2008	Supreme hitter won NL batting title with a .340 average in 2007
Troy Tulowitzki	SS	2006–present	Young shortstop consistently aiming for .300 average seasons with 100 RBIs
Larry Walker	RF	1995–2004	Canadian crusher won NL's MVP in 1997 with .366 batting average, 49 home runs, and 130 RBIs

By the Numbers

HITS	**Todd Helton** 1997–present 2,134	**WINS**	**Aaron Cook** 2002–present 63
HOME RUNS	**Todd Helton** 325	**Ks**	**Pedro Astacio** 1997–2001 749
STEALS	**Eric Young** 1993–1997 180	**SAVES**	**Brian Fuentes** 2002–2008 115

Prehistoric Traces

When Coors Field was being built, workers made an interesting discovery. During excavation of the field, near home plate, a dinosaur rib was found. This led to the naming of the Rockies' official mascot: Dinger, a purple dinosaur.

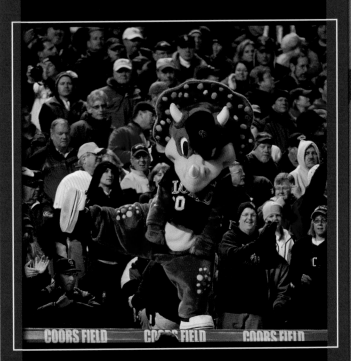

The Rockies mascot, Dinger

Into Thin Air

With the distinct quality of air in the Rockies, Coors Field is considered a hitters' park. In this stadium routine fly balls disappear over outfield walls. To counteract this effect, Rockies officials started storing their baseballs in a humidor to add moisture to the balls. They claim it's not the air's thinness that contributes to more home runs, but the air's dryness.

23

DETROIT TIGERS

Franchise Record: 8,564–8,356–93
Home Field: Comerica Park
(41,782 capacity) in Detroit, Michigan

CHAMPIONSHIPS
1935, 1945, 1968, 1984

First Season: 1901

Ever since the Tigers joined the American League as one of its charter members in 1901, baseball has been a way of life in Detroit. In 1968 the Tigers ran away with the World Series and featured the major league's last 30-game winner, pitcher Denny McLain. In 1984 the Tigers had one of the most dominant teams in major league history. That season they won 104 regular season games and posted a 7–1 playoff record on their way to a World Series win.

The 1984 Detroit Tigers

Legends & Stars

Justin Verlander

Miguel Cabrera	1B/3B	2008–present	Power hitter led the American League with 37 homers in 2008
Ty Cobb	OF	1905–1926	"The Georgia Peach" was one of the best hitters of his time, winning 11 batting titles
Hank Greenberg	1B	1930, 1933–1946	Hit 58 homers in 1938 to tie the season record at the time
Al Kaline	RF	1953–1974	Awarded 10 Gold Gloves and 15 All-Star selections in 21 seasons
Alan Trammel	SS	1977–1996	1984 World Series MVP
Justin Verlander	SP	2005–present	Hard-throwing righty posts high strikeout rates
Lou Whitaker	2B	1977–1995	An anchor at second base for 19 straight seasons and a key player in the Tigers' 1984 season

By the Numbers

HITS	**Ty Cobb** 1905–1926 3,902	**WINS**	**Hooks Dauss** 1912–1926 223	
HOME RUNS	**Al Kaline** 1953–1974 399	**Ks**	**Mickey Lolich** 1963–1975 2,679	
STEALS	**Ty Cobb** 865	**SAVES**	**Todd Jones** 1997–2001, 2006–2008 235	

Big Wins, Big Losses

In 1968 pitcher Denny McLain had a highlight season, going 31–6 with a 1.96 ERA. He also won the Cy Young and MVP awards that season. Two years later he was suspended from the league and forced into bankruptcy because of gambling. Although he was allowed to play again, he never had another winning season.

Tough Turnaround

With a record of 42–119 in the 2003 season, the Tigers set the mark for most losses in American League history. In 2006 Detroit made a major turnaround, finishing 95–67, but losing to the St. Louis Cardinals in the World Series. After trading for slugger Miguel Cabrera and pitcher Dontrelle Willis before the 2009 season, the Tigers hoped to make another World Series run. After a strong start, Detroit slipped at the end of the season and tied the Minnesota Twins for the division lead. They lost to the Twins in the 12th inning of a one-game tiebreaker and missed going to the playoffs.

Miguel Cabrera

FLORIDA MARLINS

Franchise Record: 1,283–1,403
Home Field: Land Shark Stadium
(38,560 capacity) in Miami, Florida

CHAMPIONSHIPS
1997, 2003

First Season: 1993

The Marlins began play as an expansion team in 1993. In just their fifth season, the Marlins beat the odds to capture the World Series title. The won the Series with a 3-2 victory over the Cleveland Indians in the 11th inning of Game 7. The Marlins grabbed another title in 2003 beating the New York Yankees in six games with one of the great underdog lineups in World Series history.

Josh Beckett pitched a shutout to win Game 6 of the 2003 World Series.

Legends & Stars

Josh Johnson

Josh Beckett	SP	2001–2005	2003 World Series MVP racked up 47 strikeouts in five playoff starts
Luis Castillo	2B	1996–2005	Switch-hitting speedster started on both World Series teams
Jeff Conine	OF/1B	1993–1997, 2003–2005	Balanced fielder and hitter helped Florida win both World Series
Josh Johnson	SP	2005–present	Lanky righty received first All-Star selection in 2009
Jim Leyland		1997–1998	No-nonsense manager led the Marlins to a World Series title
Hanley Ramirez	SS	2006–present	2006 NL Rookie of the Year batted .342 with 24 home runs, 106 RBIs, and 27 stolen bases in 2009
Dontrelle Willis	SP	2003–2006	High-energy hurler won the 2003 NL Rookie of the Year

By the Numbers

HITS	**Luis Castillo** 1996–2005 1,273	**WINS**	**Dontrelle Willis** 2003–2006 68 ⟶	
HOME RUNS	**Mike Lowell** 1999–2005 143	**Ks**	**Dontrelle Willis** 757	
STEALS	**Luis Castillo** 281	**SAVES**	**Robb Nen** 1993–1997 108	

New Stadium, New Name

In 2009 the Florida Marlins broke ground on a new stadium in Miami. Set to open in 2012, the stadium has a retractable roof. With the new stadium comes a new name—the Miami Marlins.

Money Flow

In just their fifth season, the Marlins shocked the baseball world by winning the 1997 World Series title. Six seasons later Florida captured another title. In between those seasons, the team's management traded its top talent to keep the budget low. But in 2008 they were able to keep shortstop Hanley Ramirez. The All-Star received a six-year contract for $70 million.

Hanley Ramirez

HOUSTON ASTROS

First Season: 1962

Baseball came to Texas in the form of the Houston Colt .45s in 1962. The team changed its name to the Astros in 1965. For 35 years they played their home games under the bubble of the Houston Astrodome to keep out the Texas heat and humidity. In 2005 the Astros nearly nabbed the World Series title but were downed by the Chicago White Sox.

Franchise Record: 3,812–3,835–5
Home Field: Minute Maid Park
(40,950 capacity) in Houston, Texas

CHAMPIONSHIPS
None

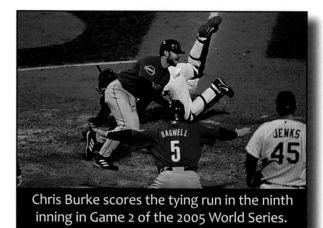

Chris Burke scores the tying run in the ninth inning in Game 2 of the 2005 World Series.

Legends & Stars

Jeff Bagwell

Jeff Bagwell	1B	1991–2005	The power-hitting "Bags" won NL Rookie of the Year in 1991 and NL MVP in 1994
Lance Berkman	1B/OF	1999–present	Power slugger has been to the All-Star Game five times
Craig Biggio	2B	1988–2007	Astros' all-time leader in hits made seven All-Star appearances and snagged four Gold Gloves
Roy Oswalt	SP	2001–present	20-game winner in both 2004 and 2005
Nolan Ryan	SP	1980–1988	Of the four teams he pitched for, Ryan was in Houston the longest, setting the team strikeout record
Mike Scott	SP	1983–1991	Went 18–10 in 1986 with a league best 2.22 ERA and 306 strikeouts on his way to a Cy Young Award
Jimmy Wynn	CF	1963–1973	Wynn's power and base-stealing ability went along with a reliable outfield glove

By the Numbers

 HITS
Craig Biggio
1988–2007
3,060

 WINS
Joe Niekro
1975–1985
144

 HOME RUNS
Jeff Bagwell
1991–2005
449

 Ks
Nolan Ryan
1980–1988
1,866

STEALS
Cesar Cedeno
1970–1981
487

SAVES
Billy Wagner
1995–2003
225

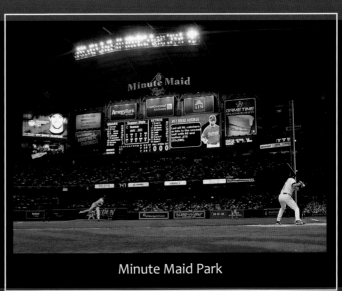

Tough Loss

The first pitcher in MLB history to lose while throwing a no-hitter was Colt .45 hurler Ken Johnson in 1964. Johnson made one of two Houston errors that allowed the Cincinnati Reds to take home a 1-0 win.

Quirky Confines

When the Astros opened Enron Field in 2000 (now Minute Maid Park), it was a unique ballpark. The $250 million price tag included a retractable roof that could open or close in 20 minutes, a foul pole on a hill inside the center field fence, and a model train that runs on 800 feet (244 meters) of track.

Minute Maid Park

KANSAS CITY ROYALS

First Season: 1969

Franchise Record: 3,143–3,360–2
Home Field: Kauffman Stadium
(38,177 capacity) in Kansas City, Missouri
CHAMPIONSHIP
1985

The Royals, along with three other teams—the Seattle Pilots, Montreal Expos, and San Diego Padres—began play in the American League in 1969. After finishing the best of the four new clubs, great success followed in the 1970s and early 1980s. The Royals captured their one and only World Series title in 1985.

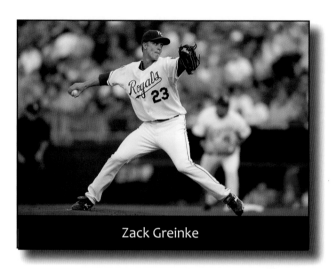
Zack Greinke

Legends & Stars

Hal McRae

George Brett	3B	1973–1993	Almost became the first player since Ted Williams to hit .400, finishing at .390 and winning the AL MVP in 1980
Billy Butler	1B	2007–present	Young first baseman is able to hit for both average and power
Zack Greinke	SP	2004–present	2009 Cy Young Award winner is on the rise
Hal McRae	OF/DH	1973–1987	Contact hitter topped .300 seven times in 15 seasons
Bret Saberhagen	SP	1984–1991	Won two Cy Young awards and a World Series MVP award in 1985 with the Royals
Frank White	2B	1973–1990	Average hitter and solid defender for 18 straight seasons
Willie Wilson	CF	1976–1990	Speedy outfielder was a threat on the base paths

By the Numbers

HITS	**George Brett** 1973–1993 3,154	**WINS**	**Paul Splittorff** 1970–1984 166
HOME RUNS	**George Brett** 317	**Ks**	**Kevin Appier** 1989–1999, 2003–2004 1,458
STEALS	**Willie Wilson** 1976–1990 612	**SAVES**	**Jeff Montgomery** 1988–1999 304

I-70 Connection

The 1985 World Series pitted the Kansas City Royals against the St. Louis Cardinals. The Missouri cities are connected by Interstate 70, so the matchup was called the I-70 series. After losing the first two games at home, the Royals won four of the last five to take the series.

Jim Sundberg slides into home for the winning run in Game 6 of the 1985 World Series.

Bizarre Pine Tar

The Royals were down 4–3 with two outs in the top of the ninth against the Yankees on July 24, 1983. George Brett came to the plate and cracked a home run and rounded the bases. But Yankees manager Billy Martin protested that Brett's bat had an illegal amount of pine tar on it. The umpires agreed and took away Brett's homer. After the game the AL commissioner reinstated the homer and ordered the rest of the game played three weeks later. The Royals went on to win 5-4.

LOS ANGELES ANGELS
of Anaheim

Franchise Record: 3,887–3,921–3

Home Field: Angel Stadium of Anaheim
(45,050 capacity) in Anaheim, California

CHAMPIONSHIP
2002

First Season: 1961

The Los Angeles Angels began play in the American League in 1961. In 1966 the team changed its name to the California Angels before renaming itself the Anaheim Angels in 1997. They finally became the Los Angeles Angels of Anaheim in 2005. Hall of Famers Rod Carew, Reggie Jackson, and Nolan Ryan spent part of their careers in Angels uniforms.

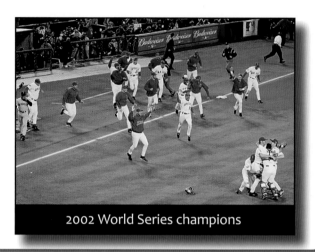

2002 World Series champions

Legends & Stars

Vladimir Guerrero

Rod Carew	1B	1979–1985	One of the best singles hitters of all time provided a spark to the Angels' lineup
Jim Fregosi	SS	1961–1971	Six-time All-Star went on to manage the club for parts of four seasons
Vladimir Guerrero	OF	2004–2009	Home run and RBI machine took home the AL MVP award in 2004
Reggie Jackson	OF/DH	1982–1986	Baseball legend led the AL in home runs in 1982 for the Angels
Nolan Ryan	SP	1972–1979	Strikeout hurler led the AL in strikeouts in six of his seven seasons with the Angels
Jered Weaver	SP	2006–present	Steady pitcher is an anchor for the Angels' rotation

By the Numbers

HITS	**Garret Anderson** 1994–2008 2,368	**WINS**	**Chuck Finley** 1986–1999 165
HOME RUNS	**Tim Salmon** 1992–2004, 2006 299	**Ks**	**Nolan Ryan** 1972–1979 2,416
STEALS	**Chone Figgins** 2002–2009 280	**SAVES**	**Troy Percival** 1995–2004 316

Quick Start

When the Angels started play in 1961, no one expected them to do much. But the team impressed, finishing the season with a 70–91 record and a .435 winning percentage—the best of any expansion club in its first season.

Wild Card Winner

In 2002 the World Series teams—the Anaheim Angels and the San Francisco Giants—were wild card teams. It was the first time both wild card teams made it to the championship series since the wild card started in 1995. The Angels and Giants battled it out for seven games, with the Angels winning it all in Game 7. The championship started a new era for the Angels, who made the playoffs six times between 2002 and 2009.

The 2002 Angels had a parade in their honor at Disneyland in Anaheim, California.

LOS ANGELES DODGERS

Franchise Record: 10,055–9,117–139

Home Field: Dodger Stadium
(56,000 capacity) in Los Angeles, California

CHAMPIONSHIPS
1955, 1959, 1963, 1965, 1981, 1988

First Season: 1884

It was on the East Coast in Brooklyn, New York, that the Dodgers originally began play in 1884. They had many nicknames in Brooklyn, including the Atlantics, Grays, Superbas, Robins, and finally, the Dodgers. In 1958 the Dodgers switched coasts and moved to Los Angeles. Since then the Dodgers have won five World Series titles.

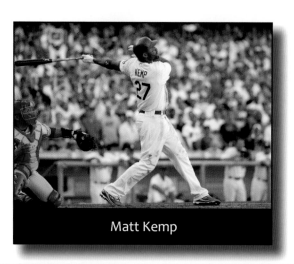
Matt Kemp

Legends & Stars

Jackie Robinson

Chad Billingsley	SP	2006–present	Solid right-hander made his first All-Star appearance in 2009
Roy Campanella	C	1948–1957	"Campy" won three NL MVP awards
Don Drysdale	SP	1956–1969	1962 NL Cy Young Award winner spent time as a Dodgers announcer after his playing career
Matt Kemp	CF	2006–present	Fast youngster steals bases, hits for average, and has a wide range in the outfield
Sandy Koufax	SP	1955–1966	Amazing career included four no-hitters, three NL Cy Young awards, an NL MVP, and four World Series titles
Pee Wee Reese	SS	1940–1942, 1946–1958	"The Little Colonel" was the Dodgers' team captain for seven NL pennant-winning teams
Jackie Robinson	2B	1947–1956	Broke MLB color barrier in 1947 as a 28-year-old rookie; won NL MVP in 1949 behind incredible speed and hitting ability

By the Numbers

HITS	Zack Wheat 1909–1926 2,804	**WINS**	Don Sutton 1966–1980, 1988 233
HOME RUNS	Duke Snider 1947–1962 389	**Ks**	Don Sutton 2,696
STEALS	Maury Wills 1959–1966, 1969–1972 490	**SAVES**	Eric Gagne 1999–2006 161

Born to Manage

Tommy Lasorda made it to the major leagues as a player. His career stats in three years included one hit in eight at-bats and an 0–4 pitching record in less than 60 innings. Lasorda turned to coaching in 1973 and managed the Dodgers to three World Series titles.

Campy's Legacy

Roy Campanella became the first catcher to break the MLB color barrier in 1948. He blossomed into one of the league's best catchers of the 1950s. But in 1958 an automobile accident paralyzed Campy from the chest down. He continued to work for the Dodgers in community relations and became an inspiration to the disabled.

Roy Campanella

MILWAUKEE BREWERS

Franchise Record 3,089–3,420–4
Home Field: Miller Park
(41,900 capacity) in Milwaukee, Wisconsin

CHAMPIONSHIPS
None

First Season: 1969

Milwaukee was one of the eight charter members of the American League in 1901, but the franchise lasted only one season there. It moved to Baltimore, where the players became the Orioles. Another franchise, the Braves, tried its hand in Milwaukee from 1953 to 1965 before moving to Atlanta. Finally, in 1970 the Milwaukee Brewers were born, a team that started as the Seattle Pilots the year before.

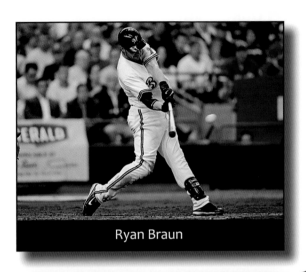
Ryan Braun

Legends & Stars

Prince Fielder

Ryan Braun	3B/LF	2007–present	Two-time All-Star who can hit for average and power is also a threat on the base paths
Prince Fielder	1B	2005–present	Power hitter slams home runs like his father, Cecil, but hits for a better average
Rollie Fingers	RP	1981–1982, 1984–1985	Closer pulled off an impressive AL Cy Young Award and AL MVP sweep in 1981
Paul Molitor	IF	1978–1992	Hall of Famer was patient at the plate, compiling a lifetime batting average of .306
Dan Plesac	RP	1986–1992	Selected to three All-Star teams as a Brewer
Robin Yount	SS	1974–1993	The AL MVP in 1982 and 1989 had a long career in Milwaukee

By the Numbers

HITS	**Robin Yount** 1974–1993 3,142	**WINS**	**Jim Slaton** 1971–1977, 1979–1983 117
HOME RUNS	**Robin Yount** 251	**Ks**	**Ben Sheets** 2001–2008 1,206
STEALS	**Paul Molitor** 1978–1992 412	**SAVES**	**Dan Plesac** 1986–1992 133

World Series Records

After a strong 1982 season, the Brewers met the St. Louis Cardinals in the championship. In Game 1 Paul Molitor set a World Series record by getting five hits in one game. Robin Yount set another record by collecting four hits in a game twice during the World Series. The records were not enough, though, as the Cardinals took the series in seven games.

Brewers catcher Ted Simmons blocks the plate against Cardinals shortstop Ozzie Smith during Game 3 of the 1982 World Series.

Piloting to Milwaukee

Though Major League Baseball had just granted Seattle a new expansion franchise in 1969, the team's ownership had major financial and stadium issues. So, after one year, future MLB commissioner Bud Selig snapped up the franchise and moved it to Milwaukee, where the Pilots became the Brewers.

MINNESOTA TWINS

Franchise Record: 8,138–8,748–109
Home Field: Target Field
(40,000 capacity) in Minneapolis, Minnesota

CHAMPIONSHIPS
1924, 1987, 1991

First Season: 1901

The Twin Cities of Minneapolis and St. Paul had minor league teams throughout the early 20th century with the Minneapolis Millers and St. Paul Saints. But Major League Baseball didn't make a home in Minnesota until 1961. The Washington Senators moved to town, and the team was renamed the Twins. Minnesota won two World Series championships in 1987 and 1991 behind center fielder Kirby Puckett.

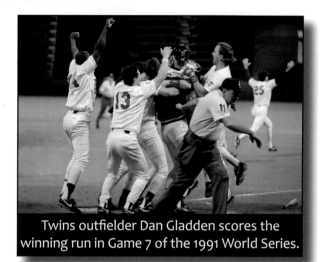

Twins outfielder Dan Gladden scores the winning run in Game 7 of the 1991 World Series.

Legends & Stars

Joe Mauer

Bert Blyleven	SP	1970–1976, 1985–1988	Strikeout pitcher with a monster curveball helped the Twins win the 1987 World Series and is now a Twins TV announcer
Kent Hrbek	1B	1981–1994	"Herbie" hit a game-winning home run in the 12th inning of his MLB debut and a grand slam in the 1987 World Series
Harmon Killebrew	1B/3B	1954–1974	"Killer" smacked home runs for the Senators and Twins during three decades
Joe Mauer	C	2004–present	With three batting titles and the 2009 AL MVP under his belt, Mauer signed with the Twins through 2018
Justin Morneau	1B	2003–present	Canadian slugger won the 2006 AL MVP
Tony Oliva	RF	1962–1976	Oliva led the AL in hits for five seasons
Kirby Puckett	CF	1984–1995	Power and average hitter also won six Gold Gloves

By the Numbers

HITS	**Sam Rice** 1915–1933 2,889	
WINS	**Walter Johnson** 1907–1927 417	
HOME RUNS	**Harmon Killebrew** 1954–1974 559	
Ks	**Walter Johnson** 3,508	
STEALS	**Clyde Milan** 1907–1922 495	
SAVES	**Rick Aguilera** 1989–1995, 1996–1999 254	

The Great Outdoors

For 27 seasons the Twins made their home inside the Hubert H. Humphrey Metrodome. But in 2010 the team began play in their new stadium at Target Field under a Minnesota sky instead of a teflon roof. The Twins' first home in Minnesota was at Metropolitan Stadium, also an outdoor park.

Target Field

A Close Call

In 2002 Major League Baseball owners voted 28–2 to eliminate two of the league's teams, targeting the Montreal Expos and Minnesota Twins. But the Twins survived thanks to the Metrodome, which would not legally let them out of their lease. That season the Twins won their division.

NEW YORK METS

First Season: 1962

Franchise Record: 3,655–3,981–8
Home Field: Citi Field
(41,800 capacity) in New York, New York

CHAMPIONSHIPS
1969, 1986

Established in 1962 through major league expansion, the New York Mets quickly built a winner. By 1969 the Mets won the World Series with a collection of players known as the "Amazin' Mets." The Mets added another title in 1986 with an incredible seven-game World Series victory over the Boston Red Sox.

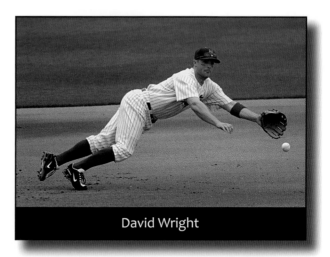
David Wright

Legends & Stars

Jose Reyes

Gary Carter	C	1985–1989	Reliable catcher was a three-time All-Star with the Mets
Dwight Gooden	SP	1984–1994	"Doc" went 17–9 in 1984 to win the NL Rookie of the Year; he won the Cy Young Award with a career-best 24–4 mark in 1985
Keith Hernandez	1B	1983–1989	Hernandez's high batting average went with six Gold Gloves
Jose Reyes	SS	2003–present	Rookie of the Year winner in 2003, the speedy shortstop led the league in stolen bases in 2006 and 2007
Tom Seaver	SP	1967–1977, 1983	Won NL Cy Young awards in 1969, 1973, and 1975
Darryl Strawberry	RF	1983–1990	1983 Rookie of the Year leads the team in home runs
David Wright	3B	2004–present	Solid third baseman is one of MLB's best young players

By the Numbers

HITS	**Ed Kranepool** 1962–1979 1,418	
HOME RUNS	**Darryl Strawberry** 1983–1990 282	
STEALS	**Jose Reyes** 2003–present 301	
WINS	**Tom Seaver** 1967–1977, 1983 198	
Ks	**Tom Seaver** 2,541	
SAVES	**John Franco** 1990–2001, 2003–2004 276	

Subway Series

Two teams from New York have met in the World Series 14 times in major league history. The most common matchups have been the Yankees versus the Brooklyn Dodgers or New York Giants. In 2000 the Yankees took on the Mets in the Subway Series. The Yankees won the highly anticipated World Series four games to one.

Yankees catcher Jorge Posada tags out Mets outfielder Timo Perez in the 2000 World Series.

Long, Slow Walk

The 1969 Mets won the World Series, but the season didn't start well. Many claim the season's turning point came during the second game of a doubleheader on July 30, 1969. Outfielder Cleon Jones failed to hustle after a ground ball. Manager Gil Hodges removed Jones from the game by walking onto the outfield to retrieve Jones himself. Although some reports claim Jones was taken out of the game because of a possible injury, the other players took notice of the manager's public display. The Mets went 45–19 to finish the season.

41

NEW YORK YANKEES

First Season: 1901

Franchise Record: 9,575–7,294–93
Home Field: Yankee Stadium
(52,325 capacity) in New York, New York

CHAMPIONSHIPS
1923, 1927, 1928, 1932, 1936, 1937, 1938, 1939, 1941, 1943, 1947, 1949, 1950, 1951, 1952, 1953, 1956, 1958, 1961, 1962, 1977, 1978, 1996, 1998, 1999, 2000, 2009

The most famous franchise in major league history started out in Baltimore in 1901 as the Orioles. Two seasons later the franchise moved to New York to become the Highlanders. In 1913 the team was renamed the Yankees, and success soon followed after Babe Ruth joined the team in 1919. The Yankees won their first World Series title in 1923 and their 27th in 2009.

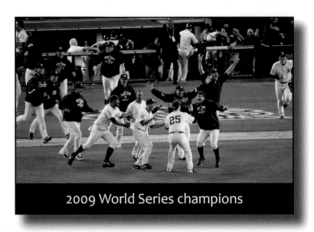
2009 World Series champions

Legends & Stars

Mickey Mantle

Yogi Berra	C	1946–1963, 1965	Famous catcher won the AL MVP in 1951, 1954, and 1955
Joe DiMaggio	OF	1936–1942, 1946–1951	"Joltin' Joe" won three MVPs and had a 56-game hit streak, a record that remains intact today
Whitey Ford	SP	1950, 1953–1967	Started the opening game of the World Series 10 times
Derek Jeter	SS	1995–present	The Yankees' hits leader has been part of five World Series championship teams
Mickey Mantle	OF	1951–1968	One of the game's greats won AL MVPs in 1956, 1957, and 1962
Mariano Rivera	RP	1995–present	The dominant closer has led the league in saves three times
Babe Ruth	OF	1920–1934	"The Sultan of Swat" led the AL in homers 10 of his 15 Yankee seasons

By the Numbers

HITS	**Derek Jeter** 1995–present 2,747	**WINS**	**Whitey Ford** 1950, 1953–1967 236	
HOME RUNS	**Babe Ruth** 1920–1934 659	**Ks**	**Whitey Ford** 1,956	
STEALS	**Rickey Henderson** 1985–1989 326	**SAVES**	**Mariano Rivera** 1995–present 526	

Murderer's Row

The 1927 Yankees fielded a lineup so stocked with sluggers that members of the press commonly referred to the first six hitters as "Murderer's Row." In their batting order, the hitters were Earle Combs (.356), Mark Koenig (.285), Babe Ruth (.356, 60 HRs, 164 RBIs), Lou Gehrig (.373, 47 HRs, 175 RBIs), Bob Muesel (.337), and Tony Lazzeri (.309).

End of a Streak

On May 2, 1939, Lou Gehrig, first baseman for the Yankees, took himself out of the lineup in a game at Detroit. When the announcer let fans know before the game that it was the first time in 2,130 games Gehrig would not be playing, the Detroit fans gave him a long ovation as he sat in the dugout and wept. He would die the following year of amyotrophic lateral sclerosis, a fatal disease that affects the nerve cells in the brain and spinal cord. ALS has become known as Lou

OAKLAND ATHLETICS

First Season: 1901

Franchise Record: 8,189–8,671–87
Home Field: Oakland-Alameda County Stadium
(35,067 capacity) in Oakland, California

CHAMPIONSHIPS
1910, 1911, 1913, 1929, 1930, 1972, 1973, 1974, 1989

As one of the eight charter members of the American League in 1901, the Athletics got their start in Philadelphia, where they played until 1954. Kansas City acquired the Athletics in 1965, followed by Oakland in 1968. The A's were at their prime in Oakland in the 1970s, when they won three consecutive titles starting in 1972.

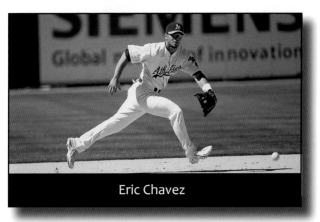
Eric Chavez

Legends & Stars

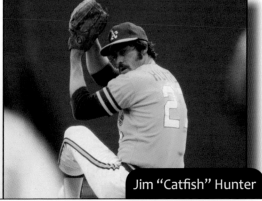
Jim "Catfish" Hunter

Eric Chavez	3B	1998–present	Slick fielder has won six Gold Gloves and can hit for power
Dennis Eckersley	RP	1987–1995	"Eck" shut down hitters in 1992, winning both the AL Cy Young and MVP
Rollie Fingers	RP	1968–1976	One of the first dominant relief pitchers in the game ensured that Oakland's final innings were in safe hands
Scott Hairston	OF	2009–present	Up-and-coming outfielder is part of a baseball-playing family line that has produced five major leaguers
Rickey Henderson	LF	1979–1984, 1989–1995, 1998	The leading base stealer in MLB history once stole 130 bases in a season (1982) and swiped an AL best 66 in 1998 at age 39
Jim "Catfish" Hunter	SP	1965–1974	The 1974 AL Cy Young Award winner was a big part of the Athletics' championship team in the early 1970s
Mark McGwire	1B	1986–1997	"Big Mac" led the A's to a World Series title in 1989

By the Numbers

HITS
Bert Campaneris
1964–1976
1,882

HOME RUNS
Mark McGwire
1986–1997
363

STEALS
Rickey Henderson
1979–84, 1989–1995, 1998
867

WINS
Eddie Plank
1901–1914
284

Ks
Eddie Plank
1,985

SAVES
Dennis Eckersley
1987–1995
320

Share and Share Alike

In the past many cities' pro stadiums supported both baseball and football teams. That's not always the case anymore. But Oakland-Alameda County Stadium still hosts the Athletics for baseball and the Oakland Raiders for football.

Oakland-Alameda County Stadium

The Mack Attack

In 1901 Connie Mack hung up his cleats as a catcher and became manager of the Philadelphia Athletics. He managed the team for the next 50 years—by far the longest run any manager has had with a team. He retired at the age of 87 with the MLB record for most wins (3,731) and games managed (7,755).

PHILADELPHIA PHILLIES

First Season: 1883

Franchise Record: 9,038–10,167–115
Home Field: Citizens Bank Park
(43,647 seats) in Philadelphia, Pennsylvania

CHAMPIONSHIPS
1980, 2008

Pro baseball showed up long ago in Philadelphia in the form of the Quakers in 1883. The franchise changed its name to the Phillies in 1890. The team briefly switched its name to the Blue Jays in 1943 and 1944 before going back to the Phillies.

2008 World Series champions

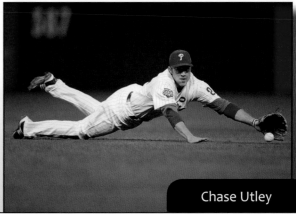

Chase Utley

Jim Bunning	SP	1964–1967, 1970–1971	Won 74 games in his first four seasons with the Phillies
Steve Carlton	SP	1972–1986	"Lefty" won NL Cy Young Award in 1972, 1977, 1980, and 1982
Ryan Howard	1B	2004–present	One of the best young sluggers in the game has already won an MVP (2006) and a World Series title (2008)
Tug McGraw	P	1975–1984	McGraw was a valuable part of many Phillies playoff teams
Robin Roberts	SP	1948–1961	Reliable starter led the NL in complete games from 1952 to 1956 and won 234 games in a Phillies uniform
Mike Schmidt	3B	1972–1989	The 10-time Gold Glove winner also earned NL MVP awards in 1980, 1981, and 1986
Chase Utley	2B	2003–present	Well-rounded threat is a four-time All-Star

By the Numbers

	Mike Schmidt 1972–1989 2,234	WINS	**Steve Carlton** 1972–1986 241
HOME RUNS	**Mike Schmidt** 548	KS	**Steve Carlton** 3,031
STEALS	**Billy Hamilton** 1890–1895 510	SAVES	**Jose Mesa** 2001–2003, 2007 112

Baseball Boones

Bob Boone, a solid catcher from 1972 to 1981 for the Phillies, has great baseball bloodlines. He is the son of major league infielder Ray Boone, who played from 1948 to 1960. He is the father of major leaguers Bret and Aaron Boone, both infielders who played in the 1990s and 2000s.

Bob Boone tags out Royals catcher Darrell Porter during Game 5 of the 1980 World Series.

Slugfest for Schmidt

In 1976 third baseman Mike Schmidt hit 12 home runs in the season's first 15 games. Four of the home runs came in a single game against the Chicago Cubs that featured 34 runs and 43 hits. With the score tied at 15 in the 10th inning, Schmidt hit his fourth home run of the game—a two-run blast—to put Philadelphia ahead for good. It was the third time in MLB history that a Phillies player hit four home runs in a game.

47

PITTSBURGH PIRATES

First Season: 1882

Franchise Record: 9,753–9,579–139
Home Field: PNC Park
(38,496 seats) in Pittsburgh, Pennsylvania

CHAMPIONSHIPS
1909, 1925, 1960, 1971, 1979

In 1882 the Pittsburgh Alleghenys became one of the first National League teams. The franchise changed its name to the Pirates in 1890 after being accused by another franchise of "pirating," or stealing, one of their best players. The nickname stuck, and the Pirates have won five World Series titles.

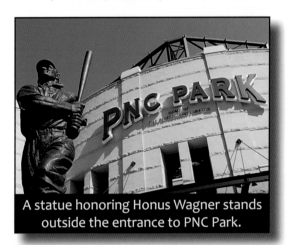

A statue honoring Honus Wagner stands outside the entrance to PNC Park.

Legends & Stars

Honus Wagner

Roberto Clemente	OF	1955–1972	Two World Series titles, four NL batting titles, and the 1966 NL MVP Award highlighted his legendary career
Garrett Jones	1B	2009–present	The first baseman slugged 21 home runs in his first season
Ralph Kiner	OF	1946–1953	Yearly contender for MVP led the NL in home runs his first seven years with the Pirates
Andrew McCutchen	CF	2009–present	Contended for NL Rookie of the Year in his first full season
Willie Stargell	1B/LF	1962–1982	"Pops" won the 1979 NL MVP award at age 39
Pie Traynor	3B	1920–1935, 1937	Hit better than .300 in 10 seasons for Pittsburgh
Honus Wagner	SS	1900–1917	"The Flying Dutchman" won an amazing eight NL batting titles in 18 seasons in Pittsburgh

By the Numbers

HITS	**Roberto Clemente** 1955–1972 3,000	**WINS**	**Wilbur Cooper** 1912–1924 202
HOME RUNS	**Willie Stargell** 1962–1982 475	**Ks**	**Bob Friend** 1951–1965 1,682
STEALS	**Max Carey** 1910–1926 688	**SAVES**	**Roy Face** 1953, 1955–1968 188

Untimely Death

At age 38 Roberto Clemente ended the 1972 season with his 3,000th hit with the Pirates. After that season he decided to help fly supplies to earthquake victims in Nicaragua. On the way the plane crashed into the Atlantic Ocean. After his death, he became the first Latin American player to be elected into the Hall of Fame.

Roberto Clemente

Most Valuable Card

In 1909 the American Tobacco Company released a set of baseball cards, but Honus Wagner, the shortstop for the Pittsburgh Pirates, objected. He didn't want his image being used for the promotion of tobacco products. His card was recalled, and in 2007 the rare 1909 Wagner card sold for $2.8 million.

SAN DIEGO PADRES

First Season: 1969

Franchise Record: 3,008–3,508–2
Home Field: PETCO Park
(42,445 capacity) in San Diego, California

CHAMPIONSHIPS
None

The Padres were established in 1969 as one of four major league expansion teams. In their 15th year in the league, they became National League champs behind the expert hitting of Tony Gwynn. The run ended short when they fell to the mighty Detroit Tigers in the 1984 World Series. The Padres again made the World Series in 1998 but lost to the New York Yankees.

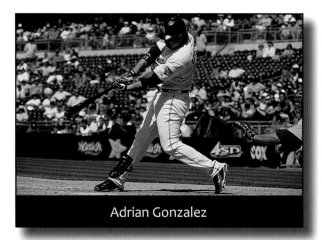
Adrian Gonzalez

Legends & Stars

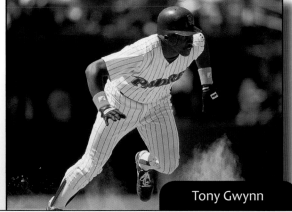
Tony Gwynn

Steve Garvey	1B	1983–1987	Veteran leader helped the Padres to the team's first World Series appearance in 1984
Adrian Gonzalez	1B	2006–present	Slugger walloped 40 home runs in 2009 All-Star season
Rich Gossage	RP	1984–1987	In four years in San Diego, "Goose" was a stopper to be reckoned with
Tony Gwynn	RF	1982–2001	Failed to reach .300 or better in only one season and collected eight NL batting titles
Randy Jones	SP	1973–1980	First great Padres hurler snagged NL Cy Young Award in 1976 with a 22–14 record and a 2.74 ERA
Dave Winfield	OF	1973–1980	Earned the first four of his 12 career All-Star appearances in a Padres uniform

By the Numbers

HITS
Tony Gwynn
1982–2001
3,141

HOME RUNS
Nate Colbert
1969–1974
163

STEALS
Tony Gwynn
319

WINS
Eric Show
1981–1990
100

Ks
Jake Peavy
2002–2009
1,348 ⟶

SAVES
Trevor Hoffman
1993–2008
552

Game Saver

In more than 15 seasons with the Padres, closer Trevor Hoffman put up Hall of Fame numbers. He racked up 552 saves in San Diego and led the majors in 1998. He has been selected for the All-Star game seven times in his career (six with the Padres) and is the all-time saves leader with 591—and counting.

Padres shortstop Khalil Greene turns a double play during the 2005 playoffs.

Worst of the Best

When the Padres won the NL's West Division with an 82–80 record in 2005, they set the MLB mark for worst record of a division winner. In the playoffs the Padres were swept in three games by the St. Louis Cardinals.

SAN FRANCISCO GIANTS

Franchise Record: 10,344–8,888–163

Home Field: AT&T Park
(41,503 capacity) in San Francisco, California

CHAMPIONSHIPS
1905, 1921, 1922, 1933, 1954

First Season: 1883

The franchise got its start in 1883 as the New York Gothams before becoming the New York Giants in 1885. The Giants were successful in New York, winning five World Series titles before the team moved to San Francisco in 1958. One of the all-time greats, Willie Mays, played 21 seasons in the Giants' orange and black.

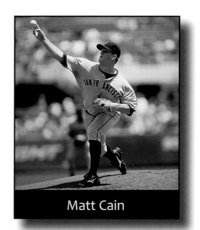
Matt Cain

Legends & Stars

Tim Lincecum

Matt Cain	SP	2005–present	Constantly improving hurler led the NL in complete games with four in 2009
Tim Lincecum	SP	2007–present	The right-hander won NL Cy Young awards in 2008 and 2009
Juan Marichal	SP	1960–1973	Won 20 games or better in six seasons as a Giant and threw an amazing 52 career shutouts
Christy Mathewson	SP	1900–1916	Won 20 games or better in 13 seasons, including four seasons with 30 or more wins
Willie Mays	CF	1951–1952, 1954–1972	"Say Hey Kid" won two NL MVP awards and 12 Gold Gloves
Willie McCovey	1B	1959–1973, 1977–1980	1959 NL Rookie of the Year went on to capture NL MVP in 1969 with a .320 average, 45 home runs, and 126 RBIs
Mel Ott	3B	1926–1947	Started in the majors at age 17 and played in 12 All-Star games

By the Numbers

HITS	**Willie Mays** 1951–1952, 1954–1972 3,187	**WINS**	**Christy Mathewson** 1900–1916 372
HOME RUNS	**Willie Mays** 646	**Ks**	**Christy Mathewson** 2,499
STEALS	**Mike Tiernan** 1887–1899 428	**SAVES**	**Robb Nen** 1998–2002 206

The Catch

In Game 1 of the 1954 World Series, the Giants and the Cleveland Indians were tied 2-2 with the Indians at bat and two men on. Cleveland's Vic Wertz hit a laser that looked as if it would easily go over the head of Giants centerfielder Willie Mays. But Mays turned on the jets and made a miraculous over-the-shoulder basket catch. The amazing play is known by baseball fans as simply "The Catch."

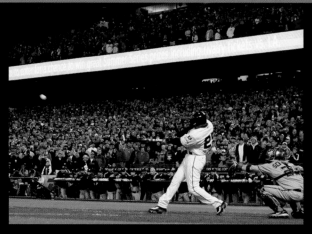

Barry Bonds hits his 756th career home run.

Barry's Bombs

Giants outfielder Barry Bonds hit the 756th home run of his career on August 7, 2007. The home run broke Hank Aaron's all-time record, but baseball fans were torn. Accusations of steroid use tainted his reputation, but many Giants fans still supported Bonds' achievement.

SEATTLE MARINERS

First Season: 1977

Franchise Record: 2,461–2,760–2
Home Field: Safeco Field
(47,116 capacity) in Seattle, Washington

CHAMPIONSHIPS
None

Seattle had much success with the Rainiers, a minor league team, going back to the start of the 20th century. In 1969 Major League Baseball awarded Seattle a pro team—the Pilots—but that team only lasted a year. Team owners moved the Pilots to Milwaukee, but Seattle got another pro team in 1977 with the Mariners.

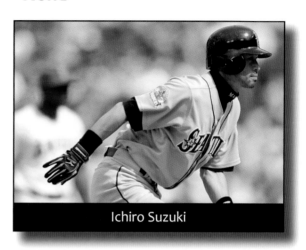
Ichiro Suzuki

Legends & Stars

Felix Hernandez

Jay Buhner	RF	1988–2001	"Bone" went to the All-Star Game and won a Gold Glove in 1996
Alvin Davis	1B/DH	1984–1991	The 1984 AL Rookie of the Year was a steady hitter in eight seasons with the Mariners
Ken Griffey Jr.	CF/DH	1989–1999, 2009–present	"Junior" was a wall-scaling centerfielder and power hitter in the '90s; his sweet swing came back to Seattle in 2009
Felix Hernandez	SP	2005–present	Intimidating power pitcher routinely racks up Ks
Edgar Martinez	3B/DH	1987–2004	Martinez made seven All-Star teams with his powerful bat
Harold Reynolds	2B	1983–1992	The Seattle speedster was a blur on the base paths and a master at turning double plays
Ichiro Suzuki	RF	2001–present	MLB's hitting machine and yearly All-Star is a threat on the base paths and in the outfield

By the Numbers

 HITS **Edgar Martinez**
1987–2004
2,247

 WINS **Jamie Moyer**
1996–2006
145

 HOME RUNS **Ken Griffey Jr.**
1989–1999, 2009–present
417

 Ks **Randy Johnson**
1989–1998
2,162

 STEALS **Ichiro Suzuki**
2001–present
341

 SAVES **Kazuhiro Sasaki**
2000–2003
129

Regular Season Success

The Mariners got the new millennium off to a great start. In 2001 they matched major league baseball's record for the most wins in a single season with 116. It hadn't been done since the Chicago Cubs set the record in 1906. But after beating the Cleveland Indians in the first round of the playoffs, the Mariners lost to the New York Yankees in the American League Championship Series.

Kingdome to Safeco

When it opened in 1976, the Kingdome in Seattle was a unique arena that eventually hosted pro baseball, football, and basketball. But by the mid-1990s, the ceiling was leaking and falling apart. The Mariners moved outdoors into Safeco Field in 1999.

Safeco Field

ST. LOUIS CARDINALS

First Season: 1882

Franchise Record: 10,019–9,342–152
Home Field: Busch Stadium
(46,861 capacity) in St. Louis, Missouri

CHAMPIONSHIPS
1926, 1931, 1934, 1942, 1944,
1946, 1964, 1967, 1982, 2006

One of baseball's oldest franchises is the St. Louis Cardinals. Formerly known as the Brown Stockings, Browns, and Perfectos, St. Louis adopted the Cardinals name in 1900. The franchise has won the second-most World Series titles in Major League Baseball history with 10.

Busch Stadium hosted the 2009 All-Star game.

Legends & Stars

Albert Pujols

Lou Brock	OF	1964–1979	Fine hitter was an even finer base stealer, leading the NL in eight seasons and setting the MLB career record at the time with 938
Dizzy Dean	SP	1930, 1932–1937	Led the NL in strikeouts four straight seasons from 1932 to 1935 and won NL MVP in 1934
Bob Gibson	SP	1959–1975	During magical 1968 season, "Hoot" won NL Cy Young Award, MVP, and Gold Glove by going 22–9 with 13 shutouts, 268 strikeouts, and a 1.12 ERA
Stan Musial	1B/OF	1941–1944, 1946–1963	"Stan the Man" was a talented hitter, winning seven NL batting titles and NL MVP in 1943, 1946, 1948
Albert Pujols	1B	2001–present	All-around hitter won the NL MVP in 2005, 2008, and 2009
Ozzie Smith	SS	1982–1996	Earned 14 All-Star selections and 13 Gold Gloves
Adam Wainwright	P	2005–present	Righty hurler had breakout season in 2009 with a 19–8 record, 212 strikeouts, and a 2.63 ERA

By the Numbers

HITS	**Stan Musial** 1941–1944, 1946–1963 3,630	**WINS**	**Bob Gibson** 1959–1975 251
HOME RUNS	**Stan Musial** 475	**Ks**	**Bob Gibson** 3,117
STEALS	**Lou Brock** 1964–1979 888	**SAVES**	**Jason Isringhausen** 2002–2008 217

Double Slam

On April 23, 1999, Cardinals third baseman Fernando Tatis became the only player in MLB history to hit two grand slams in the same inning. Chan Ho Park of the Dodgers gave up both blasts, and the Cardinals beat the Dodgers 12-5.

The Wizard

Cardinals shortstop Ozzie Smith was a fan favorite for many reasons. Besides being a Gold Glove fielder and a speedy base runner, he was known for having fun on the field. Nicknamed "The Wizard," Smith even performed backflips on special occasions when he ran to his shortstop position. He helped the team win the 1982 World Series and was inducted into the Hall of Fame in 2002.

Ozzie Smith turns a double play in the 1985 World Series against the Kansas City Royals.

TAMPA BAY RAYS

First Season: 1998

Franchise Record: 826–1,115
Home Field: Tropicana Field
(36,973 capacity) in Tampa, Florida

CHAMPIONSHIPS
None

Born as the Tampa Bay Devil Rays in 1998, the franchise was one of two new franchises that season along with the Arizona Diamondbacks. Ten years of growing pains followed. Then in 2008 the newly named "Rays" dropped the Devil from their name and recorded the first winning season in franchise history.

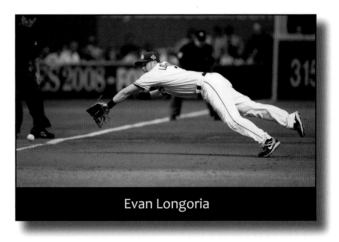
Evan Longoria

Scott Kazmir

Carl Crawford	LF	2002–present	Speedy Rays outfielder led the AL in stolen bases four times
Matt Garza	SP	2008–present	MVP for the American League Championship Series in 2008
Scott Kazmir	SP	2004–2009	Two-time All-Star led the AL in strikeouts with 239 in 2007
Evan Longoria	3B	2008–present	Power hitter won 2008 AL Rookie of the Year
Joe Maddon		2006–present	Rays' manager led his team to the 2008 World Series

By the Numbers

HITS	**Carl Crawford** 2002–present 1,296	**WINS**	**Scott Kazmir** 2004–2009 55
HOME RUNS	**Aubrey Huff** 2000–2006 128	**Ks**	**Scott Kazmir** 874
STEALS	**Carl Crawford** 362	**SAVES**	**Roberto Hernandez** 1998–2000 101

Year of Change

In 2008 when the Tampa Bay Devil Rays became the Tampa Bay Rays the team colors also changed. Black, green, and blue gave way to navy, light blue, and gold. The changes seemed to help. The 2008 Rays made the first postseason appearance in team history, finishing runner-up in the World Series to the Philadelphia Phillies.

Game 1 of the 2008 World Series at Tropicana Field

Home Field Ruckus

The Rays' home stadium, Tropicana Field, had been quiet in earlier seasons. But when Tampa Bay made the postseason in 2008, it became a place for celebration. Fans ringing cowbells made such a racket through the playoffs, it was hard to hear what was going on at the games—even on the television broadcast.

TEXAS RANGERS

First Season: 1961

Franchise Record: 3,657–4,134–6
Home Field: Rangers Ballpark in Arlington
(49,115 capacity) in Arlington, Texas

CHAMPIONSHIPS
None

Established as the expansion Washington Senators in 1961, the team became the Rangers with a move to Texas in 1972. The late 1990s was the best time to be a Rangers fan. The team won three American League West titles during that era, although they never reached the World Series.

Rangers Ballpark in Arlington

Michael Young

Juan Gonzalez	OF	1989–1999, 2002–2003	Slugger captured AL MVPs in 1996 and 1998
Josh Hamilton	OF	2008–present	Power hitter slugged 28 homers in a single round during the 2008 Home Run Derby
Ian Kinsler	2B	2006–present	2008 All-Star can hit for power and is a threat on the bases
Ivan Rodriguez	C	1991–2002, 2009	"Pudge" threw out nearly 50 percent of base runners during his career with the Rangers
Michael Young	IF	2000–present	Solid hitter and fielder gives the Rangers a veteran presence

By the Numbers

HITS	**Ivan Rodriguez** 1991–2002, 2009 1,747	WINS	**Charlie Hough** 1980–1990 139	
HOME RUNS	**Juan Gonzalez** 1989–1999, 2002–2003 372	Ks	**Charlie Hough** 1,452	
STEALS	**Bump Wills** 1977–1981 161	SAVES	**John Wetteland** 1997–2000 150	

Presidential Owner

In 1989 future U.S. President George W. Bush served as the managing general partner of the Texas Rangers. A longtime baseball fan, Bush had been a ballplayer in his youth, as had his father and grandfather.

George W. Bush delivers the ceremonial first pitch before Game 1 of the 2001 World Series.

Famous Lawmen

Since the early 1800s, the Texas Rangers have been part of state history. The lawmen dealt with some of the most infamous criminals in the United States, including John Wesley Hardin, Sam Bass, and Bonnie and Clyde. When Major League Baseball came to Arlington, Texas, in 1972, the Rangers were chosen for the pro baseball team name as a tribute to the officers.

TORONTO BLUE JAYS

First Season: 1977

Franchise Record: 2,589–2,632–3
Home Field: Rogers Field
(49,539 capacity) in Toronto, Ontario, Canada

CHAMPIONSHIPS
1992, 1993

In 1977 the Blue Jays were added to Major League Baseball's roster as an expansion team. The Blue Jays got hot in the early 1990s. All-Stars Joe Carter and Roberto Alomar Jr. led the team to back-to-back World Series titles in 1992 and 1993.

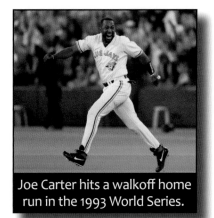
Joe Carter hits a walkoff home run in the 1993 World Series.

Legends & Stars

Aaron Hill

Roberto Alomar Jr.	2B	1991–1995	Competitive infielder was a Gold Glover and All-Star in each of his five seasons with the Jays
Jorge Bell	OF	1981–1990	Racked up 47 homers and 134 RBIs on his way to winning the AL MVP in 1987
Joe Carter	OF/DH	1991–1997	Carter's bat and leadership were key to Toronto's repeat World Series wins
Carlos Delgado	1B	1993–2004	Ball-crushing hitter was an anchor in Toronto for 12 seasons
Aaron Hill	2B	2005–present	Had breakout 2009 season with 36 home runs and 108 RBIs
Adam Lind	DH	2006–present	Slugger batted .305 with 35 home runs and 114 RBIs in 2009
Dave Steib	SP	1979–1992, 1998	Carried the Jays through much of the 1980s, pitching more than 200 innings nine times

By the Numbers

HITS	Tony Fernandez 1983–1990, 1993, 1998–1999, 2001 1,583	**WINS**	Dave Stieb 1979–1992, 1998 175
HOME RUNS	Carlos Delgado 1993–2004 336	**Ks**	Dave Stieb 1,658
STEALS	Lloyd Moseby 1980–1989 255	**SAVES**	Tom Henke 1985–1992 217

SARS Scare

When there was a breakout of Severe Acute Respiratory Syndrome in 2003, the World Health Organization warned against travel to Toronto. Hoping to show the city was safe, the Blue Jays countered by offering $1 tickets for an April home game against the Texas Rangers. The low ticket price drew more than 48,000 fans to the ballpark, a near sell-out.

Baseball or Snowball?

On April 7, 1977, the weather report in Toronto called for snow. That same day the first game in Blue Jays' history was scheduled to be played. The weather didn't stop the game—the Blue Jays took the field against the White Sox and took home a frosty 9-5 victory.

Snow covered the field during the Blue Jays' first game in 1977.

WASHINGTON NATIONALS

Franchise Record: 3,098–3,409–4

Home Field: Nationals Park
(41,888 capacity) in Washington, D.C.

CHAMPIONSHIPS
None

First Season: 1969

The forefathers of the Washington Nationals were the Montreal Expos, a major league expansion team. In 2002 Major League Baseball itself bought the Expos and three years later moved the ball club to Washington, D.C. The team was renamed the Nationals. Though the new Washington team hasn't done much winning in the nation's capital, the Nats treated fans to a beautiful new ballpark in 2008.

Nationals Park

Legends & Stars

Ryan Zimmerman (11)

Andre Dawson	OF	1976–1986	"Hawk" was 1977 NL Rookie of the Year and led the league in hits in 1983
Dennis Martinez	SP	1986–1993	"El Presidente" led the NL with a 2.39 ERA and five shutouts in 1991
Pedro Martinez	SP	1994–1997	Ace hurler won his first of three NL Cy Young awards in 1997 with the Expos
Tim Raines	LF	1979–1990, 2001	"Rock" led the NL in steals for four straight years
Tim Wallach	3B	1980–1992	Steady hitter and fielder was selected to five All-Star games
Ryan Zimmerman	3B	2005–present	Had a breakout 2009 season that included a Gold Glove, an All-Star appearance, and a 30-game hitting streak

By the Numbers

HITS	**Tim Wallach** 1980–1992 1,694	
HOME RUNS	**Vladimir Guerrero** 1996–2003 234	
STEALS	**Tim Raines** 1979–1990, 2001 635	
WINS	**Steve Rogers** 1973–1985 158	
Ks	**Steve Rogers** 1,621	
SAVES	**Jeff Reardon** 1981–1986 152	

Go Natinals, Er, Nationals!

In an April 2009 home game, two Nationals players—Adam Dunn and Ryan Zimmerman—wore jerseys with the team name across the chest misspelled "Natinals." Majestic Athletic, the jersey manufacturers, apologized for the error.

Cruel Strikes

The Montreal Expos had their two best seasons in years when baseball players went on strike. In 1981 a mid-season strike canceled 38 percent of the regular season schedule. The Expos still made the playoffs, but they lost in the NL Championship. In 1994 the Expos had baseball's best record when the season ended in August without any playoffs.

Seattle Mariners

Oakland Athletics
San Francisco Giants

Colorado Rockies

Los Angeles Dodgers
Los Angeles Angels
of Anaheim

San Diego Padres

Arizona
Diamondbacks

Texas Rangers

TEAM
MAP

Minnesota
Twins

Toronto Blue Jays

Boston Red Sox

Milwaukee
Brewers

Detroit Tigers

New York Mets
New York Yankees

Chicago Cubs

Chicago
White Sox

Cleveland
Indians

Pittsburgh
Pirates

Philadelphia Phillies

Baltimore Orioles

Washington
Nationals

Cincinnati Reds

Kansas City Royals

St. Louis Cardinals

Atlanta
Braves

Houston Astros

Tampa Bay Rays

Florida Marlins

GLOSSARY

batting average (BA)—number of hits divided by the number of at bats

Cy Young Award—award given to the best pitcher in the National League and the best pitcher in the American League each season; named after Cy Young, the major league pitcher with the most wins in pro baseball history

designated hitter—position of a player who bats each time through the batting order but does not play on defense; DHs are allowed in the American League (since 1973) but not the National League

earned run average (ERA)—used to measure how many runs a pitcher gives up every nine innings

expansion team—a new team that is added to the professional league

home run (HR)—a hit that clears the outfield wall

most valuable player (MVP) award—award given to the best National League player and best American League player each season

runs (R)—a player scores a run when he crosses home plate safely

runs batted in (RBI)—a batter receives an RBI when he drives in a run

save—statistic awarded to a relief pitcher if he enters a game with his team ahead by three or fewer runs and successfully pitches the rest of the game

strikeout (K)—when a batter receives three strikes in one at bat

BASEBALL POSITIONS

1B—first baseman

2B—second baseman

3B—third baseman

C—catcher

CF—center fielder

DH—designated hitter

IF—infielder

LF—left fielder

OF—outfielder

P—pitcher

RF—right fielder

RP—relief pitcher

SP—starting pitcher

SS—shortstop

READ MORE

Berman, Len. *The 25 Greatest Baseball Players of All Time.* Naperville, Ill.: Sourcebooks, 2010.

Burgan, Michael. *The Negro Leagues.* Mankato, Minn.: Compass Point Books, 2008.

Curlee, Lynn. *Ballpark: The Story of America's Baseball Fields.* New York: Atheneum Books for Young Readers, 2005.

Doeden, Matt. *The Greatest Baseball Records.* Mankato, Minn.: Capstone Press, 2009.

INTERNET SITES

FactHound offers a safe, fun way to find Internet sites related to this book. All of the sites on FactHound have been researched by our staff.

Here's all you do:

Visit *www.facthound.com*

Type in this code: 9781429648202

INDEX